MONSTERS

You Can Draw

Laura Pratt

AV2

www.av2books.com

Step 1
Go to **www.av2books.com**

Step 2
Enter this unique code

VLRXGRIG7

Step 3
Explore your interactive eBook!

CONTENTS

AV2 is optimized for use on any device

Your interactive eBook comes with...

Contents
Browse a live contents page to easily navigate through resources

Audio
Listen to sections of the book read aloud

Videos
Watch informative video clips

Weblinks
Gain additional information for research

Try This!
Complete activities and hands-on experiments

Key Words
Study vocabulary, and complete a matching word activity

Quizzes
Test your knowledge

Slideshows
View images and captions

... and much, much more!

2

MONSTERS

CONTENTS

MONSTERS

Monsters have been a favorite subject of moviemakers since film's earliest days. Even today, movies about vampires, werewolves, and zombies are quite popular. Every year, people flock to theaters to see these monsters wreak havoc in the world of movies.

The idea of scary creatures roaming Earth has been around for a very long time. Many **myths** from ancient Greece and Rome feature monstrous creatures not friendly to humans. Other cultures also have stories about creatures who stalk and **prey** on unsuspecting humans. Most monsters made their first appearances in literature and art.

4 YOU CAN DRAW

WHY DRAW?

triangle

circle

Sometimes, monsters are portrayed as misunderstood beings that are quite **benign** and may even be friendly. As you draw the pictures in this book, think about the reasons why authors, artists, and storytellers have created these monsters. What roles do they play in our world?

Look around you. The world is made of shapes and lines. By combining simple shapes and lines, anything can be drawn. A dragon's wing is made up of triangles with a few details added. A ghost's head can be a circle. Almost anything, no matter how complicated, can be broken down into simple shapes.

What shapes do you see in this ogre?

Meet the
CYCLOPS

Cyclopes have been described as very strong, stubborn, and violent monsters. They are a part of Greek and Roman mythology. The Cyclopes may have been brothers. They were said to be the sons of the Greek god Uranus, who was the god of the sky, and Gaia, who was the goddess of the earth. In Greek mythology, Cyclopes were so nasty and dangerous that they spent much of their lives locked away in prison.

In Greek mythology, the Cyclopes worked as the **blacksmiths** to the gods. **Legend** says that Cyclopes created the thunderbolt for Zeus, the Greek god of the sky. They also created the trident for Poseidon, the Greek god of the sea. Cyclopes were said to have made the world's volcanoes. As they spent so much of their time crafting metal weapons, Cyclopes are often pictured in a **forge**.

Size
Although Cyclopes are often imagined to look like humans, they are always shown as giants. Their massive size is part of what makes these creatures so scary.

YOU CAN DRAW

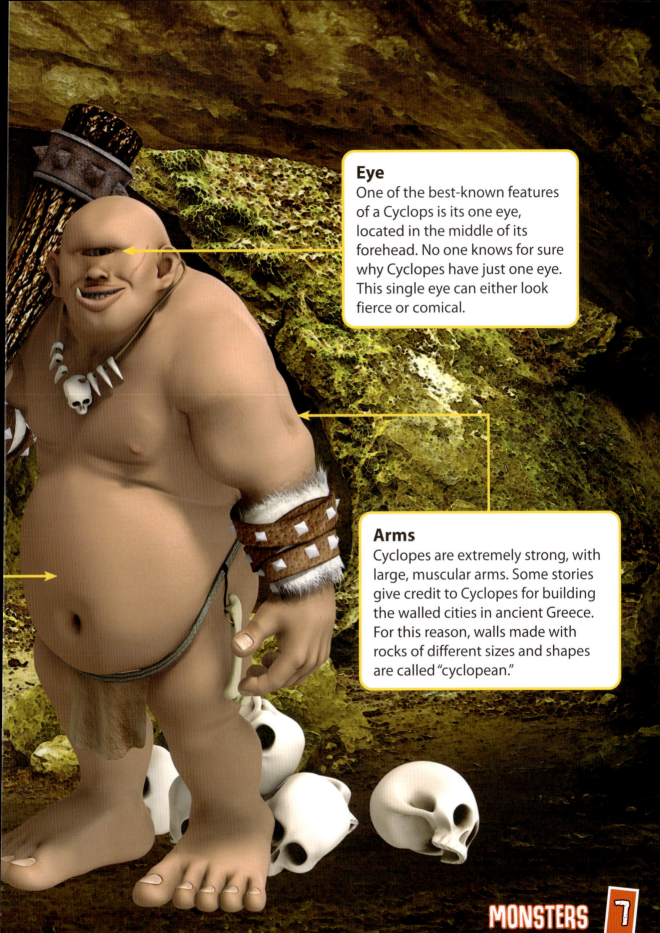

Eye

One of the best-known features of a Cyclops is its one eye, located in the middle of its forehead. No one knows for sure why Cyclopes have just one eye. This single eye can either look fierce or comical.

Arms

Cyclopes are extremely strong, with large, muscular arms. Some stories give credit to Cyclopes for building the walled cities in ancient Greece. For this reason, walls made with rocks of different sizes and shapes are called "cyclopean."

How to Draw a
CYCLOPS

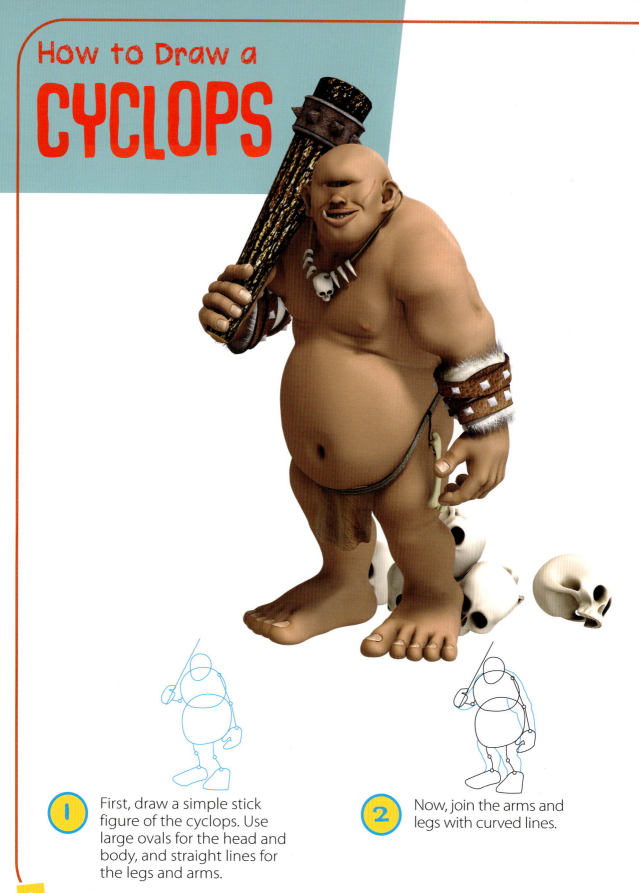

1 First, draw a simple stick figure of the cyclops. Use large ovals for the head and body, and straight lines for the legs and arms.

2 Now, join the arms and legs with curved lines.

YOU CAN DRAW

3 Next, draw the eye, ovals for the skulls, and add details to the face.

4 Next, draw his clothing.

5 In this step, draw his weapon.

6 Next, add details to the body and skulls.

7 Add more details to the weapon, skulls, and clothing.

8 Erase the extra lines and the stick figure.

9 Color the image.

Meet the
GORGON

A gorgon is a female monster from Greek mythology. The most famous gorgon is Medusa, the daughter of the sea god Phorcys. According to the poet Hesiod, Medusa was one of three gorgon sisters. She was once a beautiful **maiden**, but another goddess turned Medusa into a gorgon for lying.

According to Greek mythology, the hero Perseus killed Medusa by cutting off her head with a sword. When Medusa died, two children were born from the blood in her neck. These children were Chrysaor and Pegasus, the horse with wings.

2 The number of snake species on Earth today that contain Medusa's name.

2010

The year the film *Percy Jackson and the Olympians: The Lightning Thief*, featuring the Medusa character, was released.

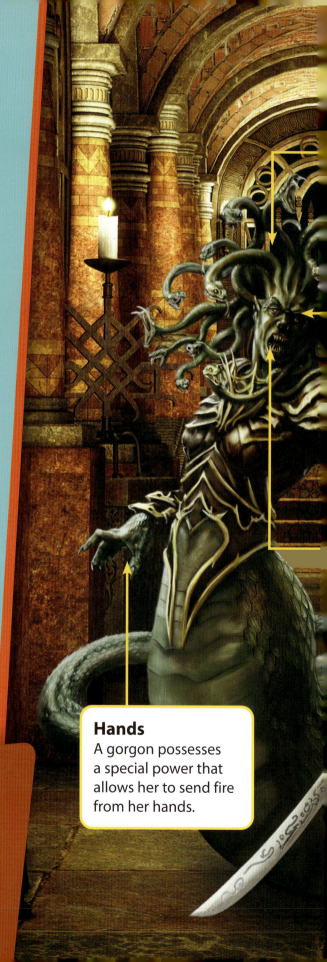

Hands
A gorgon possesses a special power that allows her to send fire from her hands.

YOU CAN DRAW

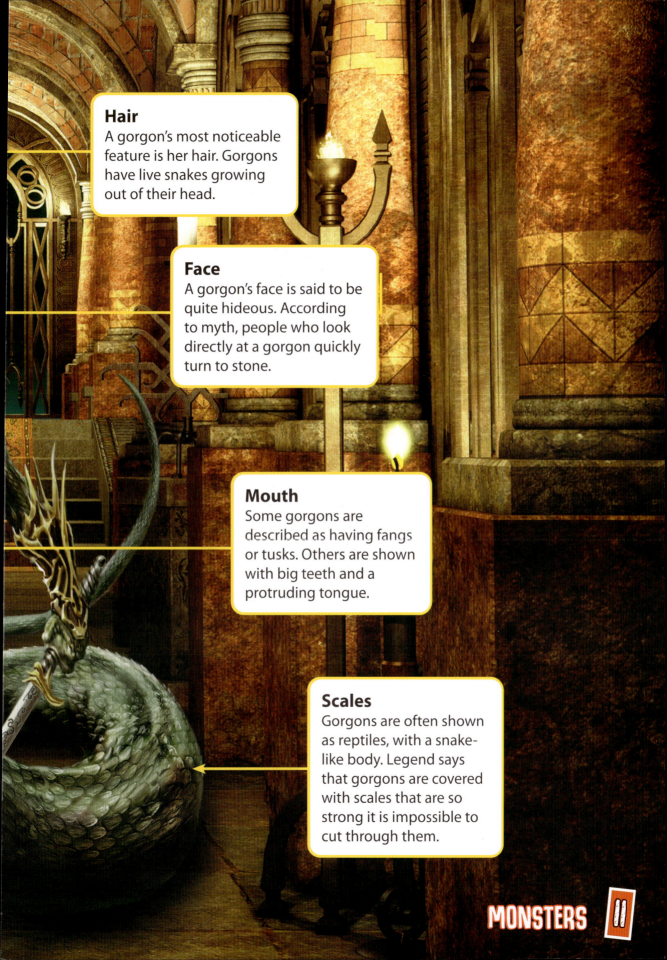

Hair
A gorgon's most noticeable feature is her hair. Gorgons have live snakes growing out of their head.

Face
A gorgon's face is said to be quite hideous. According to myth, people who look directly at a gorgon quickly turn to stone.

Mouth
Some gorgons are described as having fangs or tusks. Others are shown with big teeth and a protruding tongue.

Scales
Gorgons are often shown as reptiles, with a snake-like body. Legend says that gorgons are covered with scales that are so strong it is impossible to cut through them.

How to Draw a
GORGON

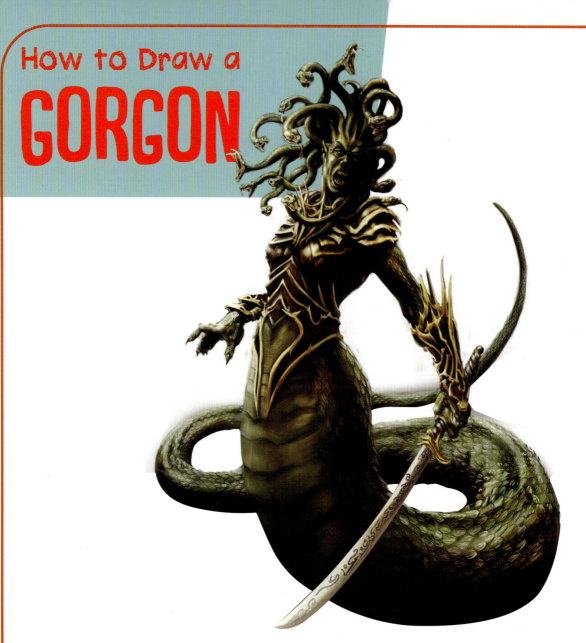

 Start with a simple stick figure of the gorgon. Draw ovals for the head and body, and lines for the hair and tail.

 Now, draw curved lines from the abdomen to form a tail.

3 Next, draw curved lines from the body for the arms.

4 Add details to the face, and draw curved lines for the hair.

5 In this step, draw the armor.

6 Draw her hands and weapon. Add more details to the armor.

7 Draw scales on the body, and add finer details to the hair.

8 Erase the extra lines.

9 Color the image.

Meet the
MUMMY

A mummy is a body that has been preserved after a person died. Mummies are usually associated with Egypt. Ancient Egyptians believed that, when a person died, his or her body traveled with the soul into the **afterlife**. For this reason, it was important that the person's body be preserved.

It was not until the late 1600s that mummies began to be portrayed as monsters. Authors began to tell stories of mummies who had risen to haunt the living. These mummies were not quite alive but not dead either.

70
The approximate number of days it took to complete the mummification process.

70 million
The estimated number of animal mummies made in Egypt over 3,000 years.

Coffin
Ancient Egyptians placed a mummy inside a coffin called a sarcophagus. Monster mummies are often shown rising from these coffins.

YOU CAN DRAW

Bandages

Mummies are popularly depicted as humans wrapped in layers of bandages. In some movies, mummies are able to remove their bandages and look like living human beings.

Resin

As mummies were being wrapped in bandages, **embalmers** used hot resin, or glue, to keep each layer of bandages in place.

Amulets

An amulet is a small object such as a necklace, ring, or bracelet. Amulets are believed to give people good luck. In ancient Egypt, amulets were placed between the layers of bandages on the dead person's body. Amulets were supposed to give the person special powers or good luck in the afterlife. Monster mummies are often shown with an amulet around their neck.

Heart

In ancient Egypt, after a person died, the body was prepared to become a mummy. Embalmers removed the brains, lungs, and other organs. The heart was left inside the body because it was considered the core of a person. This practice may have led to the belief that mummies were not actually dead.

How to Draw a
MUMMY

1 Start by drawing a stick figure of the mummy. Use ovals for the head and body, and lines for the legs and arms.

2 Now, draw curved lines to form the body and arms.

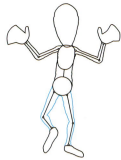

3 Draw curved lines from the abdomen to the feet to form the legs.

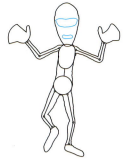

4 Next, draw ovals on the face for the eyes and mouth.

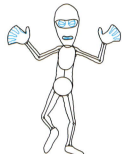

5 In this step, draw the eyes, mouth, and fingers.

6 Next, draw lines on the body to make bandages. Add detail to the eyes.

7 Add more details to the bandages on the mummy's body.

8 Erase the extra lines.

9 Color the image.

Meet the
VAMPIRE

Folklore says that a vampire is a **corpse** that has returned from the dead to steal the life force from the living. It typically does this by feeding on the blood of humans. After sucking the blood from a living creature, a vampire feels satisfied and returns to its coffin. People who have been bitten by a vampire either die from the experience or are turned into vampires themselves.

Legend says that a vampire can be killed by driving a wooden stake into its heart. Vampires are thought to be afraid of garlic. Wearing garlic can protect a person from a vampire attack.

Skin
Vampires are often described as having very pale skin. Some sources say that their skin is also very smooth, giving them a flawless **complexion**. Other sources say that a vampire's skin can look sickly due to its poor color.

Appearance
Vampires are ageless. Their appearance does not change with time. They are often depicted as charming, handsome individuals.

1732
The year the word "vampire" is believed to have first appeared in the English language.

More than 300
The number of movies made about vampires by the end of the 20th century.

YOU CAN DRAW

Eyes

Vampires' eyes might glow red and often change color when they see potential prey. Their eyes are quite sensitive to sunlight. It is said that vampires will try to avoid light sources whenever possible.

Fangs

In most stories, vampires have two fangs. They use these sharp teeth to pierce the skin of their victims before feeding on their victims' blood.

Clothing

Vampires may look like they have just returned from a dinner party. Many vampires are shown wearing black formal clothing.

How to Draw a VAMPIRE

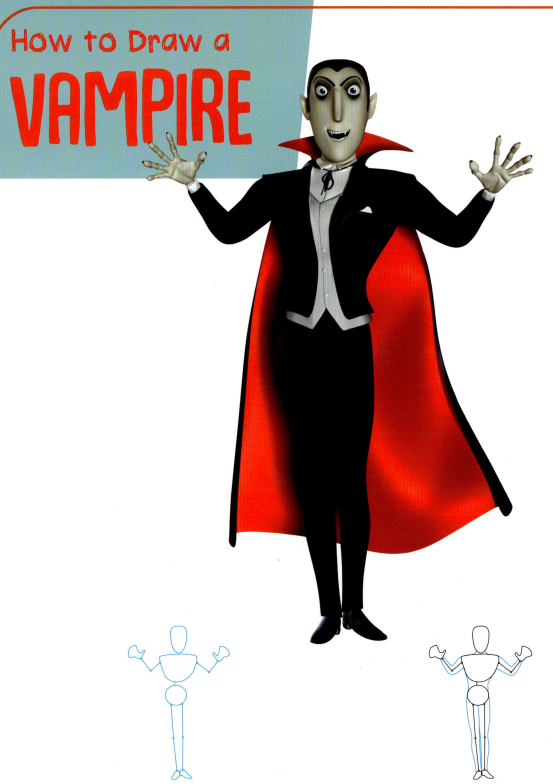

1 Start with a stick figure of the vampire. Use ovals for the head and body, and lines for the arms and legs.

2 Now, use curved lines to join the body ovals.

3 Next, start drawing the clothing.

4 Draw the eyes, ears, nose, and mouth of the vampire.

5 Add details to the clothing, and draw the hands.

6 Next, add details to the vampire's face and clothing.

7 Add finer detail to the face, hands, and clothing.

8 Erase the extra lines and the stick figure frame.

9 Color the image.

Meet the
WEREWOLF

According to folklore, a werewolf is a human who turns into a wolf at night. Werewolves are both born and created. A child born to werewolf parents may also be a werewolf. People who are bitten by a werewolf may also be turned into werewolves. Some werewolves can change between wolf and human form whenever they want to. Others change into werewolves only under a full moon. Werewolves are believed to be fast, strong, and very violent.

Werewolves usually live in forests. They spend their nights hunting humans and other animals. Killing a werewolf is a difficult task. Often, this requires a silver object, such as an silver arrow or a silver bullet. Some people believe that, if a werewolf is killed while in wolf form, it will remain a wolf forever. Others say that werewolves turn into vampires when they die.

Nose
A werewolf's face looks very much like a real wolf. Its long, pointed nose gives the werewolf a keen sense of smell.

Fur
Just like a real wolf, werewolves are covered in fur. Usually, a werewolf's fur is gray, brown, or black in color. Some people say a werewolf will have the same color of fur as its human hair.

Legs
Like a wolf, werewolves have four legs. However, werewolves walk on their back two legs like humans. Sometimes, they are shown wearing pants after they change from human to wolf form. In this case, the pants are usually ripped or torn.

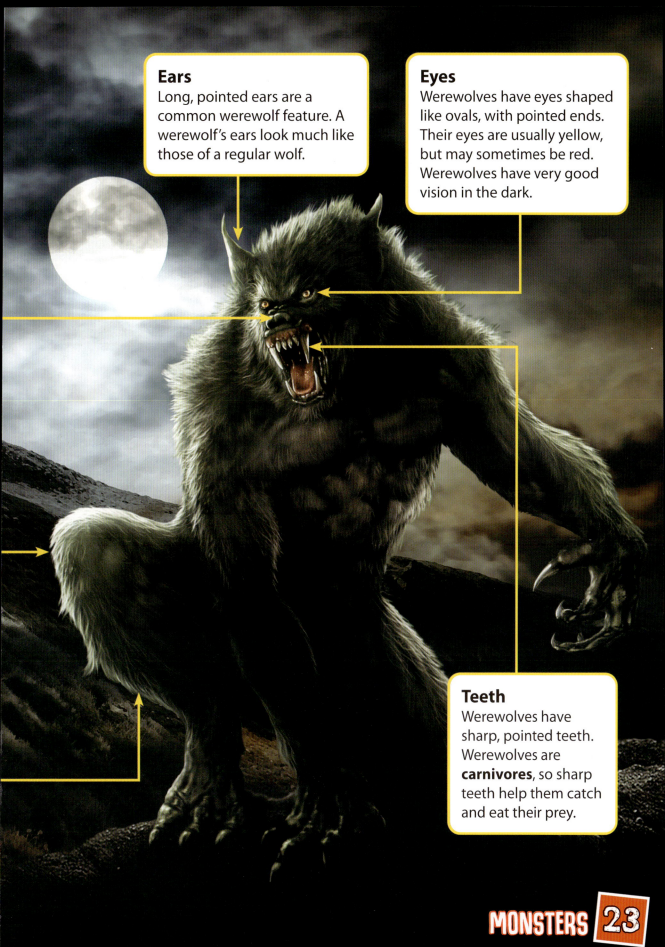

Ears
Long, pointed ears are a common werewolf feature. A werewolf's ears look much like those of a regular wolf.

Eyes
Werewolves have eyes shaped like ovals, with pointed ends. Their eyes are usually yellow, but may sometimes be red. Werewolves have very good vision in the dark.

Teeth
Werewolves have sharp, pointed teeth. Werewolves are **carnivores**, so sharp teeth help them catch and eat their prey.

How to Draw a
WEREWOLF

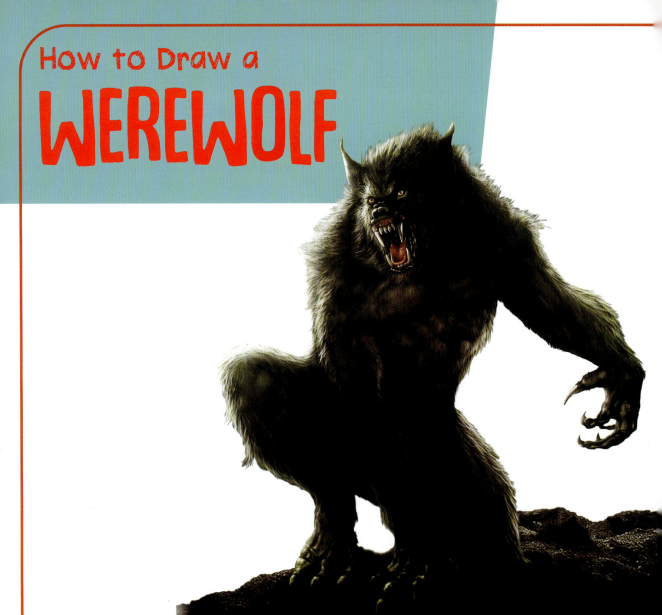

1 Start with a simple stick figure of the werewolf. Use ovals for the head and body, and lines for the arms and legs.

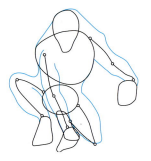

2 Now, draw curved lines over the ovals and lines to form the body.

3 Next, draw the ears, eyes, nose, mouth, hands, and feet.

4 Next, draw a line to show the ground.

5 In this step, draw fingernails on the hands and feet. Then, add the teeth.

6 Next, add details to the face, arms, hands, and feet.

7 Add fur to the werewolf's body.

8 Erase the extra lines.

9 Color the image.

Meet the
ZOMBIE

Zombies are described as the walking dead. They are thought to have escaped from their coffins. They leave the cemeteries where they were buried to search for humans. Sometimes, zombies are under the control of a master. Other times, they wander Earth without any particular direction or plan.

The legend of the zombie grew from the religious beliefs of the **voodoo culture** of Africa and Haiti. Haiti is an island in the Caribbean Sea. Voodoo folklore says that dead people can be brought back to life by the black magic of a witch doctor.

1932
The year the first zombie movie, *White Zombie*, was made.

#1
Australia's rank as the safest country to be in during a zombie outbreak.

Raised Arms
Zombies are usually seen with their arms stretched out in front of them as if they are sleepwalking.

Appearance
Zombies look like humans who are in very rough shape. As zombies have been rotting in the ground for a period of time, they often have gruesome features, such as decayed flesh and open wounds. Their clothes are also in a state of **deterioration**.

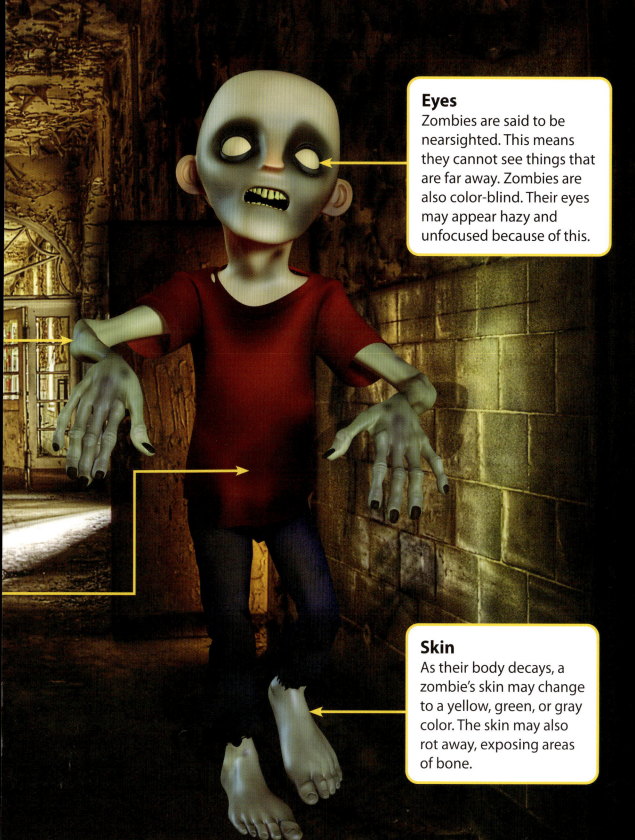

Eyes
Zombies are said to be nearsighted. This means they cannot see things that are far away. Zombies are also color-blind. Their eyes may appear hazy and unfocused because of this.

Skin
As their body decays, a zombie's skin may change to a yellow, green, or gray color. The skin may also rot away, exposing areas of bone.

How to Draw a
ZOMBIE

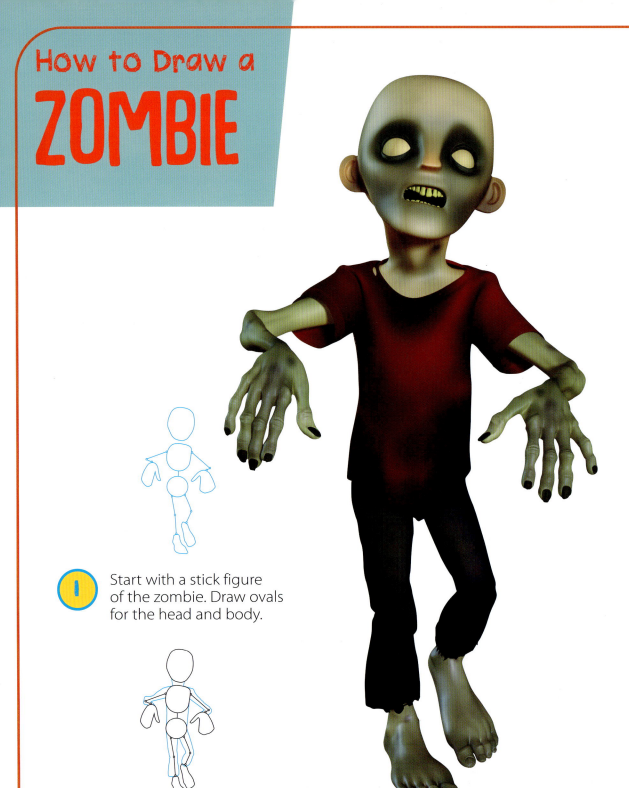

① Start with a stick figure of the zombie. Draw ovals for the head and body.

② Now, draw curved lines to form the legs, arms, and clothing.

3 Next, draw the eyes, ears, nose, and mouth.

4 Add details to the shirt.

5 In this step, draw lines on the hands and feet to form fingers and toes.

6 Draw fingernails on the hands and toenails on the feet. Add details to the face.

7 Add more details to the body.

8 Erase the extra lines.

9 Color the image.

Quiz Yourself on
MONSTERS

01 How many eyes does a Cyclops have?

02 What is the name of the best-known gorgon?

03 Which country is most associated with mummies?

04 What do you drive into the heart of a vampire to kill it?

05 Where do werewolves usually live?

06 Where did the legend of zombies come from?

07 What do gorgons have growing out of their head?

08 When were mummies first portrayed as monsters?

09 What can people wear to protect themselves from a vampire attack?

10 Which country is the safest to be in during a zombie outbreak?

30 YOU CAN DRAW

KEY WORDS

afterlife: where living creatures go after they die

benign: harmless

blacksmiths: craftsmen who make and repair things with iron

carnivores: animals that eat meat

complexion: the natural appearance of a person's skin

corpse: a dead body

deterioration: the process of a condition becoming steadily worse

embalmers: people who treat a dead body with special chemicals to preserve it from decay

folklore: a collection of traditional beliefs and stories

forge: a blacksmith's workshop

legend: an unverified story handed down from earlier times, usually believed to be based on history

maiden: a young, unmarried woman

myths: ancient stories dealing with supernatural beings and heroes

prey: to hunt and catch for food, or an animal that is hunted and caught for food

voodoo culture: a religious group that practices magic

INDEX

Get the best of both worlds.

AV2 bridges the gap between print and digital.

The expandable resources toolbar enables quick access to content including **videos**, **audio**, **activities**, **weblinks**, **slideshows**, **quizzes**, and **key words**.

Animated videos make static images come alive.

Resource icons on each page help readers to further **explore key concepts**.

Published by AV2
350 5th Avenue, 59th Floor
New York, NY 10118
Website: www.av2books.com

Library of Congress Cataloging-in-Publication Data
Names: Pratt, Laura, author.
Title: Monsters / Laura Pratt.
Description: New York, NY : AV2, [2021] | Series: You can draw | Includes
   index. | Audience: Ages 10-12 | Audience: Grades 4-6 |
Identifiers: LCCN 2019050481 (print) | LCCN 2019050482 (ebook) | ISBN 9781791119911 (library binding) | ISBN 9781791119928
   (paperback) | ISBN 9781791119935 | ISBN 9781791119942
Subjects: LCSH: Monsters in art--Juvenile literature. | Drawing--Technique--Juvenile literature.
Classification: LCC NC825.M6 P73 2021 (print) | LCC NC825.M6 (ebook) |
   DDC 741.5/37--dc23
LC record available at https://lccn.loc.gov/2019050481
LC ebook record available at https://lccn.loc.gov/2019050482

Printed in Guangzhou, China
1 2 3 4 5 6 7 8 9 0   24 23 22 21 20

042020
101319

Project Coordinator: Heather Kissock
Designer: Terry Paulhus

View new titles and product videos at www.av2books.com